萬卷文庫
61

英語散文集錦

吳奚眞 譯

Table of Contents

目　錄

On the Exercise of One's Mental Perception

by Plutarch[1]

THE mere outward sense, being passive in responding to the impression of the objects that come in its way[2] and strike upon it, perhaps cannot help entertaining and taking notice of everything that address it, be it what it will, useful or unuseful; but in the exercise of his mental perception, every man, if he chooses, has a natural power to turn himself upon all occasions, and to change and shift with the greatest ease to what he shall himself judge desirable. So that it becomes a man's duty to pursue and make after[3] the best and choicest of everything, that he may not only employ his contemplation, but may also be improved by it. For as that colour is most suitable to the eye whose freshness and pleasantness stimulates and strengthens the

心智能力的運用

我們的外部的感官，因為對於所接觸的各種事物的
印象只能被動地發生反應，所以對於外界事物向它所提
供的任何景象或聲音，不論有用也罷，無用也罷，也許
都無法不加以接納或注意；但是，在心智能力之運用之
中，每一個人——如果他願意那樣做的話——都具有一
種天生的能力，可以隨時避開某些事物，而把自己的心
思極其輕易地轉移到他認為應該加以注意的東西上面。
所以，一個人應該去追求最美好最有價值的事物，對它
加以深思熟慮，而且從這種深思熟慮之中獲得進益。一
種顏色如果能夠憑它的鮮麗與悅目來刺激並且加強人的
目力，這種顏色對於眼睛是最為適宜的；同樣地，我們

sight , so a man ought to apply his intellectual perception to such objects as with the sense of delight,
are apt to call it forth, and allure it to its own
proper good and advantage. Such objects we find
in the acts of virtue, which also produce in the
minds of mere readers about them an emulation[4]
and eagerness that may lead them on to imitation.

的心智能力也應該用於那些能夠在引起快感之中，對我們的心智能力加以發揚並有適當裨益的事物上面。這種事物就是美德的行為；單憑美德行為的記述，就足以引起讀者的一種見賢思齊之感，促使他們效法。

The Golden Mean[1]

by Balthasar Gracian[2]

A sage once reduced all virtue to the golden mean. Push right to the extreme and it becomes wrong; press all the juice from an orange and it becomes bitter. Even in enjoyment never go to extremes.

You should learn to seize things not by the blade, which cuts, but by the handle, which saves you from harm: especially is this the rule with the doings of your enemies. A wise man gets more use from his enemies than a fool from his friends. Their ill will often levels mountains of difficulties which one would otherwise not face······Flattery is more dangerous than hatred because it covers the stains which the other causes to be wiped out. The wise will turn ill will into a mirror more faithful than

中庸之道

一位聖人曾把一切美德都歸於中庸之道。如果把對的推到極端，對的就會變成錯的；如果把橘子的汁液完全榨盡，橘子就會變為苦澀。即使在享樂方面，也不要走極端。

你應該學會，在拿東西的時候不可執着鋒刃，因為鋒刃會把你割傷，而要執着把柄，因為把柄可以使你免受傷害：對於你的敵人的所做所為，尤其要實施這項規則。一個智者從他的敵人們所得到的益處，要比一個愚人從他的朋友們所得到的益處為多。他們的惡意常能促使我們克服重重的困難，而如果沒有那種惡意的激勵，我們將不能勇敢地承當那些困難。⋯⋯阿諛比仇恨更為危險，因為前者把人的污點掩飾起來，而後者卻促使那些污點都被抹消。智者把惡意化為一面比親善更為忠實

kindness, and remove or improve the faults referred to.

Everyone would have excelled in something if he had known his strong point. Notice in what quality you surpass, and take charge of that. In some, judgment excels, in others valor. Most <u>do vio- lence to</u>[3] their natural aptitude and thus attain superiority in nothing. Time disillusions us too late of what first flattered the passions.

的鏡子，並且把有關的錯誤加以消除或改進。

　　任何一個人如果曉得自己的長處，都會在某一方面有優異表現。先要認清究竟自己的哪一種本質比別人強，然後便儘量加以充實和發揮。有些人具有出眾的判斷力，有些人則勇敢過人。大多數人都戕害了他們的天賦才能，因而在任何方面都不能達到卓越的地步。等到我們從最先迎合自己的熱情的事物所造成的迷夢之中醒悟過來的時候，為時已經太遲了。

On the Instability of Human Glory

by Daniel Defoe[1]

WHAT then is the work of life? What the business of great men, that pass the stage of the world in seeming triumph as these men we call heroes have done? Is it to grow great in the mouth of fame[2] and take up[3] so many pages in history? Alas! that is no more than making a tale for the reading of posterity till it turns into fable and romance. Is it to furnish subjects to the poets, and live in their immortal rhymes as they call them? that is,in short, no more than to be hereafter turned into ballad and song and be sung by old women to quiet children, or at the corner of the street to gather crowds in aid of the pickpocket and the poor. Or is their business rather to add virtue and piety to their glory, which alone will pass them into

論人間榮譽之虛渺

　　那麼，人生的工作是什麼呢？世間的偉大人物們，像那群被稱爲英雄的人們那樣得意揚揚地走過了世界的舞臺，他們所做的事情是什麼呢？難道就是要在衆口喧騰之中變爲偉大，在歷史上佔據那麼許多篇幅嗎？唉！那也不過是造成一個故事，供後世閱讀，直至變成了神話或傳奇罷了。難道就是要供給詩人們以吟詠的題材，生活在他們的所謂不朽的詩篇之中嗎？說起來那也不過是在將來化爲歌謠，由老太婆唱給凝神靜聽的兒童，或由賣唱人在街角唱出，吸引大批的聽衆，使扒手和窮人多了一個謀生機會而已。他們所應做的事情，是不是要爲自己的榮耀添加上美德和虔誠呢？只有這兩樣東西才

eternity[4] and make them truly immortal? What is glory without virtue? A great man without religion is no more than a great beast without a soul. What is honour without merit? And what can be called true merit but that which makes a person be a good man as well as a great man?

可以使他們進入永生，真正不朽啊。沒有美德的榮耀算什麼呢？一個不奉行宗教信仰的偉人，無異於一隻沒有靈魂的巨獸。沒有價值存乎其中的榮譽算什麼呢。而可以被稱為真實價值的東西，除了那種不僅使一個人成為偉人，並且使他成為好人的本質之外，還有什麼呢？

Monuments in Westminster Abbey[1]

by Joseph Addison[2]

WHEN I look upon the tombs of the great, every motion of envy dies in me; when I read the epitaphs of the beautiful, every inordinate desire[3] goes out; when I meet with the grief of parents upon a tombstone, my heart melts with compassion; when I see the tomb of the parents themselves, I consider the vanity of grieving for those whom we must quickly follow. When I see kings lying by those who deposed them[4], when I consider rival wits[5] placed side by side. or the holy men that divided the world with their contests and disputes, I reflect with sorrow and astonishment on the little competitions, factions, and debates of mankind. When I read the several dates of the tombs, of some that died yesterday, and some six hundred years

西敏寺的墓碑

當我瞻仰偉人的墳墓的時候，一切羨慕的心情都化為烏有；當我閱讀美女的碑銘的時候，一切非非之想都離我而去；當我看見父母在愛子墓前所表現的悲痛的時候，我的心中充滿同情；當我看到父母本身的墳墓的時候，我便覺得為了那些我們不久即須相隨於地下的人們而憂傷，實屬徒然無益。一些帝王和那些把他們趕下王位的人們並排而臥，敵對的才子們在地下成為比鄰，由他們的爭端和歧見而使世界四分五裂的宗教領袖們相伴長眠——當我看到這些情景的時候，我不禁懷着憂愁和驚愕的心情，想到人世間的許多競爭、傾軋和辯論實在無謂得很。當我逐一瀏覽那些墓碑——有些墓碑標着昨天的日期，有些墓碑標着六百年前的日期——上的日期

ago, I consider <u>that great day</u>[6] when we shall all of us be contemporaries, and make our appearance together.

的時候，我不禁想到末日審判，在那個日子來臨的時候，
我們大家都將聚首一堂，成為同時代的人了。

Affectation¹

by Lord Chesterfield²

MOST people complain of fortune, few of nature³; and the kinder they think the latter has been to them, the more they murmur at what they call the injustice of the former.

Why have not I the riches, the rank, the power, of such and such? is the common expostulation with fortune; but why have I not the merit, the talents, the wit, or the beauty of such and such others? is a reproach rarely or never made to nature.

The truth is, that nature, seldom profuse, and seldom niggardly, has distributed her gifts more equally than she is generally supposed to have done. Education and situation make the great difference. Culture improves, and occasions elicit, nat-

矯　飾

大多數人都抱怨命運，卻很少有人抱怨造物；他們越覺得後者厚待他們，越對他們所謂的前者的不公做不平之鳴。

爲什麼我就沒有某某人那樣的財富，地位，權力呢？這是人們常向命運提出的抗議；但是爲什麼我就沒有另外的某某人那樣的優良資質，才能，機智，或美呢？這種譴責，人們卻很少或從來不曾向造物提出過。

實際的情形是，造物既不常豪奢，也很少慳吝，她對於天賦的分配，比一般人所設想的更爲平均。教育和境遇造成了很大的差別。天賦的才能，可以由敎化而增進，也可以爲機緣所觸發。

ural talents.

If sometimes our common parent has been a little partial, and not kept the scales quite even; if one <u>preponderates</u>[4] too much , we throw into the lighter a due <u>counterpoise</u>[5] of <u>vanity</u>[6], which never fails to set all right. Hence it happens, that hardly any one man would, without reserve, and in every particular, change with another.

Though all are thus satisfied with the dispensations of nature, how few listen to her voice! how few follow her as a guide! In vain she points out to us the plain and direct way to truth; vanity, fancy, affectation, and fashion, assume her shape, and wind us through fairyground to folly and error.

These deviations from nature are often attend-

如果造物主有時稍微偏袒一些，沒有把天平弄得十分平衡；如果某人的分量過重，我們就在較輕的一邊放上適量的自負，做爲砝碼，這種東西永遠能夠產生平衡的功效。因此，沒有一個人願意毫無保留地而且在所有方面同任何旁人互相交換。

雖然所有的人們都這樣地對造物的分配感覺滿意，可是真能聽從造物的意旨的人，真能追隨她的領導的人，卻何其稀少！她向我們指出通往真實的明白而直接的道路，但是沒有用：自負、愛好、矯飾、和風尚都假裝她的形體出現，領着我們曲曲折折地通過了一個虛幻境界，而終於導致愚蠢和錯誤。

這些背離自然的行徑時常會產生一些嚴重的後果，

ed by serious consequences, and always by ridiculous ones; for there is nothing truer than the trite
observation[7], "that people are never ridiculous for
being what they really are, but for affecting what
they really are not." Affectation is the only source,
and, at the same time, the only justifiable object, of
ridicule.

而且永遠會產生一些可笑的後果，因為有一句老話說，
「人們在保持本來面目的時候，絕對不會是可笑的；只
有在裝腔做態的時候，他們才是可笑的，」這句話實在
是最眞實不過的。矯飾是招致嘲笑的來源，而且也是嘲
笑的唯一的適當對象。

Comparison

by David Hume[1]

THAT there is a natural difference between merit and demerit, virtue and vice, wisdom and folly, no reasonable man will deny:yet it is evident that, in affixing the term, which denotes either our approbation or blame, we are commonly more influenced by comparison than by any fixed unalterable standard <u>in the nature of things</u>[2]. In like manner, quantity, and extension, and bulk, are by every one acknowledged to be real things:but when we call any animal great or little, we always form a secret comparison between that animal and others of the same species; and it is that comparison which regulates our judgment concerning its greatness. A dog and a horse may be of the very same size, while <u>the one</u>[3] is admired for the greatness of

比　較

在長處和短處、美德和罪惡、智慧和愚蠢之間，自然有其不同之處，這是任何有理性的人都不會否認的。可是在把這樣的一個表示稱讚或責難的字樣加給某人的時候，通常最能影響我們的判斷的往往是一種比較，而不是合乎事物之常理的任何確定不移的標準。同樣地，數量、範圍、和體積，都被大家認為是真實的東西：但是當我們說任何一個動物是大或小的時候，我們總是把那個動物和同類的其他份子暗中做一比較；而左右着我們關於它的大小所做的判斷的，乃是那番比較。一隻狗和一匹馬可能是一樣大小的，可是前者會因其身軀的大

its bulk, and <u>the other</u>[4] for the smallness. When I present, therefore, at any dispute, I always consider with myself whether it be a question of comparison or not that is the subject of controversy; and if it be, whether the disputants compare the same objects together, or talk of things that are widely different.

而受讚賞，後者則因其身軀的小而受誇獎。所以，當我參加任何爭辯的時候，我總是要考慮一下，爭辯的主題是不是一個比較的問題；如果是的話，我還要考慮，爭辯者是在把同類的東西放在一起加以比較呢，還是在談論一些彼此大不相同的事物。

National Prejudices

by Oliver Goldsmith[1]

AMONG all the famous sayings of <u>antiquity</u>[2], there is none that does greater honour to the author, or affords greater pleasure to the reader (at least if he be a person of a generous and benevolent heart), than that of <u>the philosopher</u>[3], who, being asked what "countryman he was," replied, that he was, "a citizen of the world." ——How few are there to be found in modern times who can say the same, or whose conduct is consistent with such a <u>profession</u>[4]!——We are now become so much Englishmen, Dutchmen, Spaniards, or Germans, that we are no longer citizens of the world; so much the natives of one particular spot, or members of one petty society, that we no longer consider ourselves as the general inhabitants of the globe, or members

民族偏見

　　一位古代的哲學家在被詢問「他是哪一國的人」的時候，他回答說他是「世界的公民」。在古聖先賢所遺留下來的一切名言之中，最能使作者受人尊敬，最能為讀者（至少是對於一個秉性高潔仁愛為懷的讀者）帶來快樂的，莫過於這句嘉言。——可是，當今之世，能夠說出這個話的，或者其行為能夠與這種表白相符合的人，卻何其罕見！——我們現在都已成了十足的英國人、法國人、荷蘭人、西班牙人，而不再是世界的公民；都已變成了十足的某一個地方的人，或某一小社會的份子，而不再認為自己是整個地球的居民，或那個包括全人類

of that grand society which <u>comprehends</u>[5] the whole human kind.

<u>Did these prejudices prevail</u>[6] only among the meanest and lowest of the people, perhaps they might be excused, as they have few, if any, opportunities of correcting them by reading, travelling, or conversing with foreigners; but the misfortune is, that they infect the minds, and influence the conduct, even of our gentlemen; of those, I mean, who have every title to <u>this appellation</u>[7] but an exemption from prejudice, which however, in my opinion, ought to be regarded as the characteristical mark of a gentleman; for let a man's birth be ever so high, his station ever so exalted, or his fortune ever so large, yet if he is not free from national and other

的大社會的份子。

　　如果這些偏見僅僅流行於最微賤的人們之間，也許還情有可原，因爲他們很少有讀書、旅行、或與外國人談話的機會，因而無從糾正自己的孤陋；但是不幸的是，這些偏見甚至已經感染了我們的上流人士的心靈，影響着他們的行爲；我所說的這批上流人士，乃是指着那些除了未能免除偏見之外，在其他任何方面對於「上流人」這個頭銜都可當之無愧的人們，而在我看來，不懷偏見卻應該被視爲一個上流人的典型標誌；因爲不論他的門第如何高貴，地位如何出衆，財富如何豐盛，如

prejudices, I should <u>make bold</u>[8] to tell him, that he had a low and vulgar mind, and had no just claim to the character of a gentleman. And in fact, you will always find that those are most apt to boast of national merit, who have little or no merit of their own to depend on; than which, to be sure, nothing is more natural:the slender vine twists around the sturdy oak, for no other reason in the world but because it has not strength sufficient to support itself.

果他不能免除民族的或其他的偏見，我要冒昧地告訴他
說，他的心地卑陋，沒有資格躋身於上流人之列。那些
自己沒有長處可資依賴的人，往往最喜歡誇耀民族的優
點；這種情形實在是最爲自然的現象——細長的藤蔓之
所以纏繞着強壯的橡樹，並沒有別的理由，只因爲它沒
有足夠的力量來支持自己。

On the Fear of Death

by William Hazlitt[1]

PERHAPS the best cure for the fear of death is to reflect that life has a beginning as well as an end. There was a time when we were not[2]: this gives me no concern——why then should it trouble us that a time will come when we shall cease to be[3]? I have no wish to have been alive a hundred years ago, or in the reign of Queen Anne[4]? Why should I regret and lay it so much to heart[5] that I shall not be alive a hundred years hence, in the reign of I cannot tell whom?

To die is only to be as we were born; yet no one feels any remorse, or regret, or repugnance, in contemplating this last idea. It is rather a relief and disburthening[6] of the mind: it seems to have been a holiday time with us then: we were not called to

談怕死

克服怕死心理的最好辦法，也許是要想到人生不僅有終結，也有開端。本來我們並未生存於世間，這個事實並不使我們憂慮，那麼，我們為什麼要為了將來有一天自己會停止生存而煩惱呢？我既然不希望自己在一百年前，或在安女王的朝代活在世上，為什麼就要為了自己在一百年後不知哪位皇帝在位的朝代，不能仍然活在世上而抱憾，而耿耿於懷呢？

死亡只是恢復誕生前的原狀而已；在想到誕生前的情形時，我們都毫無悔恨、遺憾、或厭惡之感，反而覺得輕鬆解脫，那個時候彷彿是我們所度過的一段假期，

appear upon <u>the stage of life</u>[7], to wear robes or tat-
ters, to laugh or cry, be hooted or applauded; we
had lain <u>perdus</u>[8] all this while, snug out of harm's
way; and had slept out our thousands of centuries
without wanting to be waked up; at peace and free
from care, in a long <u>nonage</u>[9], in a sleep deeper and
calmer than that of infancy, wrapped in the softest
and finest dust. And the worst that we dread is,
after a short fretful, feverish being, after vain
hopes, and idle fears, to sink to final repose again,
and forget the troubled dream of life!

我們還沒有被召出現在人生舞臺之上，或身着華服，或衣衫襤褸，或笑，或哭，或遭叫囂反對，或受喝采讚揚；在那個時候，我們一直高臥在虛無之境，無人聞問，舒適而又安全；我們在長眠中度過了千百世紀，不希望被人喚醒，一直逍遙於一個漫長的渾渾噩噩的時期之中，享受着一場比嬰兒時代的更爲深沈而平靜的睡眠，覆蔽在最輕柔最微小的塵屑之中，安安靜靜，無憂無慮。然後，我們在人世度過了一段短暫、煩躁、而熱狂的生活，曾經抱着種種虛空的希望，懷着種種無益的恐懼，現在所最怕的事情，卻是再度沈入那種最後的安息，和忘記人生的煩惱的夢境！

Companionship of Books

by Samuel Smiles[1]

A good book may be among the best of friends. It is the same today that it always was, and it will never change. It is the most patient and cheerful of companions. It does not turn its back upon[2] us in times of adversity or distress. It always receives us with the same kindness: amusing and instructing us in youth, and comforting and consoling us in age.

Books possess an essence of immortality. They are by far[3] the most lasting products of human effort. Temples and statues decay, but books survive. Time is of no account[4] with great thoughts, which are as fresh today as when they first passed through their author's minds, ages ago. What was then said and thought still speaks to us as vividly as ever from the printed page. The only effect of

與書籍爲友

一本好書可以成爲我們的最好的朋友。它過去怎樣，現在仍是怎樣，而且將來永遠不會改變。它是一個最有耐心而愉快的友伴。在我們遭遇逆境和困苦的時候，它不會不理我們。它永遠以同樣的親切態度來接待我們：在青年時期，愉悅和教導我們，在老年時期，慰藉我們。

書籍具有一種不朽的本質。它們是人類努力的一種最持久的產物。廟宇和偶像不免頹毀，但是書籍永遠存在。時間對於偉大的思想是毫無影響的，在今天，那些偉大的思想仍然像許多年前它們湧現在作者心靈之中的時候同樣新鮮。作者當年所說的話和所想的事情，現在仍然像過去同樣生動地從印刷的篇幅傳送到我們的心靈之中。時間對於書籍的唯一作用，是把不好的作品加以

time has been to sift out the bad products; for nothing in literature can long survive but what is really
good.

Books introduce us into the best society; they
bring us into the presence of the greatest minds[5]
that have ever lived. We hear what they said and
did; we see them as if they were really alive; we
sympathize with them, enjoy with them, grieve with
them; their experience becomes ours, and we feel as
if we were in a measure[6] actors with them in the
scenes which they describe.

淘汰；因為在文學的園地之中，除非是真正美好的作
品，絕對不能長久存在。

　　書籍引導我們和最優秀的人士晤聚；書籍把我們帶
到那些最偉大的曠世的才智之士的面前，我們傾聽他們
所說的話和所做的事情；我們看見他們，好像他們真的
活在世上一般；我們和他們發生同感，與他們同享樂，
共憂苦；他們的經驗變成了我們的經驗，我們覺得自己
彷彿就是在他們所描述的一幕一幕的戲劇當中和他們共
同表演的演員。

The Cynic[1]

by Henry Ward Beecher[2]

THE Cynic is one who never sees a good quality in a man, and never fails to see a bad one. He is the human owl, vigilant in darkness and blind to light, mousing for[3] vermin, and never seeing noble game[4].

His criticisms and innuendoes[5] fall indiscriminately upon every lovely thing like frost upon flowers. If Mr. A. is pronounced a religious man, he will reply: yes, on Sundays. My.B. has just joined the church: certainly, the elections are coming on. The minister of the gospel is called an example of diligence: it is his trade. Such a man is generous: of other men's money. This man is obliging to lull suspicion and cheat you. That man is upright, because he is green[6].

犬儒主義者

一個犬儒主義者是怎樣的人呢？他永遠看不見旁人的好處，卻絕對不會忽略旁人的壞處。他是一個具有人形的貓頭鷹，在黑暗之中明察秋毫，面對着光明便不見輿薪，專事搜尋鼠、鼬、蚤、蝨之類，對於高尚的獵物卻熟視無睹。

他的批評和諷刺不分皂白地降落在每一樣美好的事物上面，像嚴霜降落在花上一般。如果甲先生被宣稱是一個篤信宗教的人，他會回答說：是的，在禮拜天。乙先生剛剛加入了教會：當然嘍，選舉就要舉行了嘛。傳佈福音的牧師被稱爲勤勉的範例：那是他的行業。某人很慷慨：慷他人之慨。這個人很親切謙恭：那是爲了消除猜疑，來欺騙你。那個人是正直的：因爲他初出茅廬。

Thus his eye strains out every good quality, and takes in only the bad. To him religion is hypo-cris, honesty a preparation for fraud, virtue only want of opportunity,and undeniable purity, ascet-icism.

It is impossible to indulge in such habitual severity of opinion upon our fellow-men, without injuring the tenderness and delicacy of our feelings. A man will be what his most cherished feelings are. If he encourage a noble generosity, every feeling will be enriched by it; if he nurse bitter and envenomed thoughts, his own spirit will absorb the poison, and he will crawl among men as a burni-shed adder, whose life is mischief, and whose errand is death.

　　就是這樣地，他的眼睛濾除了一切好的性質，只吸納壞的性質。在他看來，宗教是偽善，誠實是欺騙的準備，美德只是沒有機會，無可否認的純潔只是一種苦修。

　　經常對於旁人持着這樣刻薄的看法，其結果必然損害了我們自己感情當中的親切和體貼。一個人最珍視什麼樣的感情，他就會成為什麼樣的人。如果他鼓勵一種高貴的寬宏大度，每一種情緒都將因而變得更為豐美；如果他培養刻薄惡毒的念頭，他自己的精神也將吸收其中的毒素，他將像一條有光澤的蝮蛇一般爬行於人們之間，這種蛇的生命本身就是一種禍害，它的任務是造成死亡。

He who hunts for flowers will find flowers; and he who loves weeds will find weeds.

Let it be remembered that no man, who is not himself morally diseased, will have a relish for disease in others. Reject, then, the morbid ambition of the Cynic, or cease to call yourself a man.

　　尋覓花朵的人將找到花朵；喜愛雜草的人將找到雜
草。

　　大家要記得，任何一個人，除非他本身在道德上有
毛病，絕不會津津樂道旁人的毛病。那麼，放棄犬儒主
義者的病態的雄圖罷，否則你就不要再自稱是一個人。

Riches

by Henry Ward Beecher[1]

BUT I warn you against thinking that riches
necessarily confer happiness; or that poverty con-
fers unhappiness. Do not begin life supposing that
you shall be heart-rich when you are purse-rich. A
man's happiness depends primarily upon his dispo-
sition. If that be good, riches will bring pleasure;
but only vexation if that be evil. To lavish money
upon shining trifles, to make an idol of one's self
for fools to gaze at, to rear[2] mansions beyond our
wants, to garnish them for display and not for use,
to chatter through the heartless rounds of pleasure,
to lounge, to gape, to simper and giggle——can
wealth make vanity happy by such folly? ···But
riches indeed bless that heart whose almoner[3] is
benevolence. If the taste is refined, if the affections

財　富

但是我警告你不要認爲財富一定會爲人帶來幸福，
貧窮一定會爲人帶來不幸。不要自始就存着一種想法，
以爲只要荷包豐滿，快樂自然隨之而來。一個人的快樂
幸福，主要是靠着他的性情。如果他的性情善良，財富
會爲他帶來快樂；但是如果他的性情邪惡，財富只會爲
他帶來煩惱。浪費金錢去購買種種富麗堂皇而無實際價
值的物品；把自己裝點得偶像一般，使無知之徒艷羨讚
歎；興建超過需求的華廈，加以裝潢修飾，不爲實用，
只求炫耀；沈迷於逸樂之中，終日喋喋；優閒懶散，張
口傻笑──財富能夠藉着這些愚行而使那些虛度人生之
輩快樂嗎？……但是財富的確能爲一顆仁慈爲懷的心帶

are pure, if conscience is honest, if charity listens to the needy, and generosity relieves them; if the public-spirited hand fosters all that embellishes and all that ennobles society——then is the rich man happy.

來幸福。如果情趣高尚，感情純潔，良心磊落，對於貧
困的人們充滿同情，慷慨地予以協助；如果熱心公益，
所作所為都能光耀社會，發揚人性——在這種情形之
下，富人才是快樂的。

Poverty

by Henry Ward Beecher[1]

ON the other hand, do not suppose that poverty is a waste and howling wilderness[2]. There is a poverty of vice——mean, loathsome, covered with all the sores of depravity. There is a poverty of indolence——where virtues sleep and passions fret and bicker[3]. There is a poverty which despondency makes——a deep dungeon in which the victim wears hopeless chains. May God save you from that!······But there is a contented poverty, in which industry and peace rule; and a joyful, hope, which looks out into another world where riches shall neither fly nor fade. This poverty may possess an independent mind, a heart ambitious of usefulness, a hand quick to sow the seed of other men's happiness and find its own joy in their enjoyment······If

貧　窮

在另一方面，不要以爲貧窮就是一片荒蕪淒涼的曠野。有一種貧窮代表罪惡——卑劣，可厭，滿佈着墮落的各種傷痛。有一種貧窮象徵怠惰——美德銷聲匿跡，只見情欲飛揚跋扈於其間。有一種貧窮是由沮喪所造成——當事人置身其中，有如戴着一副無法脫除的桎梏，被關在地牢裏面。願上帝保佑你，不要陷入那些貧窮之中！……但是也有一種知足常樂的貧窮，身歷其境者勤勉不懈，心安理得，懷着愉快的希望，矚望着另外一個國度，在那個國度裏面，財富既不會飛馳而來，也不會消逝無踪。如果一個人具有獨立意志，不爲流俗所左右，宅心仁厚，志在做出一些有益人群之事。隨時隨地撒播一些種子，爲旁人造成幸福快樂，而自己也樂在其中，則他必會安於這種貧窮。……如果上帝使你有機會發

God open to your feet the way of wealth, enter it cheerfully; but remember that riches bless or curse you, as your own heart determines. But if, circumscribed by necessity, you are still indigent after all your industry, do not scorn poverty. There is often in the hut more dignity than in the palace——more satisfaction in the poor man's scanty fare than in the rich man's <u>satiety</u>[4].

財，大可欣然受之；但是要記住，財富可以爲你之福，
也可以爲你之禍，完全取決於你自己的意念。但是，如
果迫不得已，你雖然勤勉不懈，而仍然不免貧乏，你也
不必輕蔑貧窮。茅屋陋舍之中，常比華廈巨邸裏面具有
更多的高貴尊嚴；窮人的粗茶淡飯，也往往比富人的酒
肉饜飽更能使人感到滿足。

The Time Is Short

by Philips Brooks[1]

YOU who are letting miserable misunderstandings <u>run on</u>[2] from year to year, meaning to clear them up some day; you who are keeping wretched quarrels alive because you cannot quite make up your mind that now is the day to sacrifice your pride and kill them; you who are passing men sullenly upon the street, not speaking to them out of some silly spite, and yet knowing that it would fill you with shame and remorse if you heard that one of those men were dead tomorrow morning; you who are letting your friend's heart <u>ache for</u>[3] a word of appreciation or sympathy——if only you could know and see and feel, all of a sudden, that "the time is short" how it would <u>break the spell</u>[4]! How you would go instantly and do the thing which you might never have another chance to do !

人生幾何

　　有些人，任憑一些不幸的誤會繼續存在，年復一年，打算等將來再行澄清；有些人，任憑一些可憐的爭執繼續爲害，因爲他們不能下定決心，現在就犧牲自己的自尊心，消除那些嫌隙；有些人，在大街上遇見某些人的時候，由於某種愚蠢的怨恨，故意繃着臉，不同他們講話，但是自己心裏也明白，如果在明天早晨聽說其中的某一個人，離開了人世，自己的心中一定充滿了羞愧和悔恨之情；有些人，吝惜一句讚賞或同情的話，而使朋友渴望着——只要你們憬悟到「人生幾何」，就會胸襟開朗，不再沈迷於那些無謂的計較。你會馬上去做一些現在不做以後也許就永遠沒有機會做的事情。

Irony[1] and Pity

by Anatole France[2]

THE more I think of the problems of our lives, the more I am persuaded that We ought to choose Irony and Pity for our assessors and judges as the ancient Egyptians called upon the <u>Goddess Isis</u>[3] and the <u>Goddess Nephthys</u>[4] on behalf of their dead.

Irony and Pity are both <u>of good counsel</u>[5]; the first with her smiles makes life agreeable; the other sanctifies it with her tears.

The Irony which I invoke is no cruel Deity. She mocks neither love nor beauty. She is gentle and kindly disposed. Her mirth disarms and it is she who teaches us to laugh at rogues and fools, whom <u>but for</u>[6] her we might be so weak as to despise and hate.

諷刺與悲憫

我 越思索人生的各種問題，越認為我們應該選擇「諷刺」和「悲憫」作為我們的裁判者，正像古代埃及人要求艾西斯女神和奈夫蒂斯女神對他們的死者所做的一樣。

諷刺和悲憫都是我們的良師益友；前者以她的微笑使人生適意；後者以她的眼淚使人生化為神聖。

我所祈求的諷刺並不是一個殘酷的神靈。她既不嘲笑愛，也不嘲笑美。她的性情是溫婉而仁慈的。她的歡樂可以解除對方的武裝。教我們嘲笑惡棍和傻瓜的就是她；要不是有她的指引，我們將會脆弱得對那批人加以輕蔑和憎恨。

Man and Nature

by Hamilton Wright Mabie[1]

THE intimacy between man and Nature began with the birth of man on the earth, and becomes each century more intelligent and far- reaching. To Nature, therefore, we turn[2] as to the oldest and most influential teacher of our race; from one point of view once our task- master, now our servant; from another point of view, our constant friend, instructor, and inspirer. The very intimacy of this relation robs it of a certain mystery and richness which it would have for all minds if it were the reward of the few instead of being the privilege of the many. To the few it is, in every age, full of wonder and beauty; to the many it is a matter of course. The heavens shine for all, but they have a changing splendor to those only who see in every

人與自然

人與自然之間的親密關係，自從世界有人類的時候就已開始，而且不斷地發揚光大，每一世紀都進展得比以前更爲明智而廣遠，所以，我們求助於自然，視之爲人類的最年長最有影響力的老師；從某一個觀點來看，它一度是我們的監工，現在卻成了我們的僕役；從另一個觀點來看，它是我們的忠實的朋友，教導者和啓發者。這種親密的關係，如果僅是少數人的報酬，而非多數人的榮幸，便會在一切人的心目中具有一種神祕和情趣，但是事實上，這種親密關係既爲普天之下的人們所共享，親密已使這種關係失去了那種神祕和情趣。對於少數人，這種關係在每一個時代都充滿了奇妙和美；對於多數人，它只是當然之事。有些人，在每一個午夜的天空都能看出一種蘊含着創造性的能力與憑藉的莊嚴肅穆之美，不論那種景象重複多少次，都不會使那種美模糊不清。天空爲一切人而照耀，但是只有在那些人的心目

midnight sky a majesty of creative energy and resource which no repetition of the spectacle can dim. If the stars shone but once in a thousand years, men would gaze, awe- struck and worshipful, on a vison which is not less but more wonderful because it shines nightly above the whole earth. In like manner, and for the same reason, we become indifferent to that delicately beautiful or sublimely impressive sky scenery which the clouds form and reform, compose and dissipate, a thousand times on a summer day. The mystery, the terror, and the music of the sea; the secret and subduing charm of the woods, so full of healing for the <u>spent</u>[3] mind or the restless spirit; the majesty of the hills, holding in their recesses the secrets of light and atmosphere;

中具有一種變化多端的壯麗。如果星辰每一千年才照耀
一次，人們將懷着敬畏尊崇的心情凝視那種美景，而那
種美景如果夜夜在全世界的上空出現，不但不會減損，
反而更爲增加它的奇妙。同樣地，而且由於同一的理由，
我們對於夏日天空的那種由浮雲聚散飄忽所造成的一日
之間千變萬化的纖巧秀麗或壯麗動人的景色，也都漠然
置之。自然界隨處都是一些可以使人生豐美的奇異景
物；海洋的神祕、恐怖、和音樂；極善於醫療疲憊心靈
和煩躁精神的森林所具有的奧妙和懾人魂魄的魔力；在
其幽深之處保有光與大氣之奧祕的山巒，所呈現的莊嚴

the infinite variety of landscape, never imitative or repetitious, but always <u>appealing</u>[4] to the imagination with some fresh and <u>unsuspected</u>[5] loveliness; ——who feels the full power of these marvellous resources for the enrichment of life, or takes from them all the health, delight, and enrichment they have to bestow?

肅穆之美；從不模仿或重複，而永遠以一種出人意表的
新鮮的美麗來訴諸人類想像的風景，所顯示的變幻無
窮；──有誰感受到這些奇異景物的全部力量，或取得
了它們所要賜與的一切健康、快樂、和豐美呢？

The Mission of the Motion Picture

by Thomas Alva Edison[1]

I consider that the greatest mission of the motion picture is first to make people happy, to bring more joy and cheer and wholesome good will into this world of ours. And God knows we need it. Second ——to educate, and inspire. I believe that the motion picture is destined to revolutionize our educational system, and that in a few years it will supplant largely, if not entirely, the use of textbooks in our schools. Books are clumsy methods of instruction at best[2], and often even the words of explanation in them have to be explained. I should say that on the average[3] we get only about two per cent efficiency out of school books as they are written today. The education of the future, as I see it, will be conducted through the medium of the motion

電影的使命

我認爲電影的最大使命，第一是使人們快樂，爲我們這個世界帶來更多的歡喜，愉悅，和有益的善意。上帝知道我們需要這種東西。第二是教育人們，使人們向上，並且對人們有所啓發。幾年之內，學校裏面的教科書將大部分（如果不是全部的話）被電影所取代。書籍充其量只是一種笨拙的教學工具，甚至其中的解釋的字句往往還必須加以解釋。我可以說，平均講來，我們從目前這種教科書所獲得的效率，僅僅約達百分之二。據我看，將來的教育要藉着電影這種工具進行，也可以說

picture, a visualized education, where it should be possible to obtain a one hundred percent efficiency. The motion picture has tremendous possibilities for the training and development of the memory. There is no medium for memory- building as productive as the human eye. That is another basic reason for the motion picture in the school. It will make a more alert and more capable generation of citizens and parents. You can't make a trained animal unless you start with a puppy. It is <u>next to</u>[4] impossible to teach an old dog new tricks. I do not believe that any other single agency of progress has the possibilities for a great and permanent good to humanity that I can see in the motion picture. And those possibilities are only beginning to be touched.

是成爲一種視覺化的教育，在那種情形之下，教育可能
達到百分之百的效率。對於記憶力的訓練和培養，電影
可能發生鉅大的效果。最能建立記憶的媒介物，莫過於
人類的眼睛。這是電影之所以應該用於學校的另一個基
本理由。它將會造成一代更機警更能幹的公民和父母。
想把一隻動物訓練好，非從幼小的時候開始不可。教老
狗學新把戲，幾乎是不可能的事。我相信，任何其他一
種進步的助力，都不能具有像我在電影身上所預見到的
那些可能的效果，藉以達成人類的一種鉅大而永久的利
益。而對於那些可能的效果，我們現在不過剛剛開始談
到而已。

We Are on a Journey

by Henry Van Dyke[1]

WHEREVER you are, and whoever you may be, there is one thing in which you and I are just alike at this moment, and in all the moments of our existence. We are not at rest[2]; we are on a journey. Our life is a movement, a tendency, a steady, ceaseless progress towards an unseen goal. We are gaining something, or losing something, everyday. Even when our position and our character seem to remain precisely the same, they are changing. For the mere advance of time is a change. It is not the same thing to have a bare field in January and in July. The season makes the difference. The limitations that are childlike[3] in the child are childish[4] in the man.

Everything that we do is a step in one direction

我們是在旅途中

不論你在何處，不論你是何人，在此時此刻，以及在我們一生當中的每時每刻，你和我有一點是完全相同的。那就是：我們不是處於靜止狀態，我們是在一個旅途之中。我們的生活是朝着一個看不見的目標而前進的一項活動，一個趨勢，或一項穩定而不停止的進展。我們每天都在增加一些東西，或失去一些東西。即使在我們的地位和品性似乎仍和過去毫無二致的時候，它們也是在變化着。因為單單時間的進展就是一種改變。同樣地保有一片荒田，在一月裏就和在七月裏不同。季節造成了差別。兒童的一些缺陷，被視為天真無邪，如果表現在成人的身上，就是幼稚。

我們所做的每件事情都是朝着某個方向邁進的一

or another. Even the failure to do something is in itself a deed. It sets us forward or backward. The action of the negative pole of a magnetic needle is just as real as the action of the positive pole. To decline is to accept——the other alternative.

Are you nearer to your port toady than you were yesterday? Yes,——you must be a little nearer to some port or other; for since your ship was first launched upon the sea of life, you have never been still for a single moment; the sea is too deep, you could not find an anchorage if you would; there can be no pause until you come into port.

步。甚至未做某件事情。這個事實本身也是一項行為。
它使我們前進一些，或後退一些。磁針的陰極的作用，
是和陽極的作用同樣實際的。拒絕就是接受——不過是
另外的一個代替的途徑而已。

　　你今天是否比昨天更為接近你的港口呢？是的，
——你一定會稍微更為接近某一港口的；因為自從你的
船第一次在人生之海洋中下水的時候起，你從來不曾停
息片刻；這個海洋太深了，縱然你想尋找一個停泊之
所，也不可得；在未駛進港口之前，你是不能停頓的。

The Strenuous Life

by Theodore Roosevelt[1]

A life of slothful ease, a life of that peace which springs merely from lack either of desire or of power to strive after great things, is as little worthy of a nation as an individual.

We do not admire the man of timid peace. We admire the man who embodies victorious efforts, the man who never wrongs his neighbor, who is prompt to help a friend, but who has those virile qualities necessary to win in the stern strife of actual life. It is hard to fail, but it is worse never to have tried to succeed. In this life we get nothing save[2] by effort. Freedom from effort in the present merely means that there has been effort stored up in the past. A man can be freed from the necessity of work only by the fact that he or his fathers

艱辛的人生

一種怠惰安逸的生活，一種僅僅由於缺少追求偉大事物的願望或能力而造成的悠閒生活，不僅非個人所應有，亦為國家所不取。

我們不欽佩那種怯懦閒逸的人。我們欽佩那種表現出勝利的努力的人，那種永不屈待鄰人，隨時熱心幫助朋友，但是也具有那些剛健的性質，足以在實際人生的嚴酷鬥爭中獲得勝利的人。失敗是難堪的，但是永遠不曾努力爭取成功，卻更為要不得。在此生之中，任何收穫都要憑着努力爭取，才能得到。在目前不須做任何努力，只是意味着有過去的努力積儲在那裏。唯有一個人或他的祖先曾經努力工作過，得到了豐富的收穫，他才

before him have worked to good purpose³. If the freedom thus purchased is used aright, and the man still does actual work, though of a different kind, whether as a writer or a general, whether in the field of politics or in the field of exploration and adventure, he shows he deserves his good fortune.

But if he treats this period of freedom from the need of actual labor as a period, not of preparation, but of mere enjoyment, even though perhaps not of vicious enjoyment, he shows that he is simply a cumberer on the earth's surface; and he surely unfits himself to hold his own place with his fellows, if the need to do so should again arise. A mere life of ease is not in the end a very satisfactory life,

可以不必工作。如果他能把這樣換取到的自由加以正當
的運用，仍然做些實際的工作，雖然那些工作是屬於另
一類的，不論是作一名作家還是一名將軍，不論是在政
界還是在探險和冒險方面做些事情，他都表明了他沒有
辜負自己的好運。

　　但是，如果他把這段不須從事實際勞作的自由時
期，不用於從事準備，而僅僅用於享樂（雖然他所從事
的也許並不是邪惡的享樂），那就表明了他只是地球表
面上的一個贅疣；而且他一定不會有能力在同儕之中維
持自己的地位，如果那種需要再度出現的話。光是安逸
的生活終歸並不是很令人滿意的生活，而且，最重要的

and, above all , it is a life which ultimately unfits those who follow it for serious work in the world.

As it is with the individual, so it is with the nation. It is a base untruth to say that happy is the nation that has no history. <u>Thrice</u>[4] happy is the nation that has a glorious history. Far better it is to dare mighty things, to win glorious triumphs, even though checkered by failure, than <u>to take rank with</u>[5] those poor spirits who neither enjoy much nor suffer much, because they live in the gray twilight that knows neither victory nor defeat.

是，過那種生活的人最後終必無力擔當世間的嚴肅工
作。

　　個人如此，國家亦然。有人說一個沒有歷史的國家
是得天獨厚的，這是卑鄙的不實之言。一個具有光榮歷
史的國家，是非常得天獨厚的。冒險犯難去從事偉大的
事業，贏得光榮的勝利，即使其中夾雜着失敗，遠勝於
與那些既沒有享受多大快樂也沒有遭受多大病苦（因爲
他們生活在一個既沒有勝利也不會失敗的灰暗境界之
中）的凡庸之輩爲伍。

Concentration

by George Allardice Riddell[1]

THE success of some men bewilders those around them because they never seem to work, or to work for any length of time. Their secret is their power to concentrate, and thus to obtain the maximum of result with the minimum of apparent effort. "Concentration" , says Emerson, "is the secret of success in politics, in war, in trade, in short in all the management of human affairs."

Concentration is a habit of mind. Men are not born equal in their power of concentration any more than[2] in their power of playing billiards. But up to a point every one can improve his powers in every direction. This is the age of specialists. Remember that concentration is necessary not only to do things, but to select what to do. In these days[3] no one can achieve great distinction unless he

專　心

有 些人似乎從來不工作，或一連工作相當長的時間，而結果竟能獲得成功，這種情形常使周遭的人們大惑不解。實際上，他們的成功祕訣在於能夠專心，因而能藉着最低限度的明顯努力，獲致最高限度的成果。愛默生說：「在政治上，在戰爭上，在商業上，以及在一切人類事務的處理上，專心都是成功的祕訣。」

專心是心靈的一種習慣。在專心的能力方面，人們並非生來完全一樣，正如在玩撞球的能力方面，也不是大家生來完全相同。但是，每個人都可以把自己的能力朝着任何一個方向增進到某種程度。目前是一個專家的時代。要記住，不僅做事情的時候需要專心，在選擇所要做的事情的時候也需要專心。在目前這個時代，一個

concentrates on some one thing.

It must be remembered that concentration is an exhausting mental and physical business for those who are unaccustomed to it. Therefore, to begin with, the strain should not be too prolonged. Attention should be relaxed for a suitable period. In other words the habit should be gradually formed. Brisk, vigorous concentration for a quarter of an hour on the first day may be gradually expanded into two hours or more at the end of a month. The essence of concentration is that the full powers of the mind should be centered on the task <u>in hand</u>[4]. A tired mind and body cannot accomplish this to the best advantage, and in the case of children and young persons harm may result from too prolonged efforts.

人如果不專心於某一件事情，便不會有卓越的成就。

　　我們不可忘記，對於那些尚未習慣於此道的人們，專心乃是一項使人心力交瘁的事情。所以，第一，不可把專心的緊張狀態繼續太久。應該把注意力鬆弛一個相當的期間。換句話說，這種習慣是要逐漸養成的。在第一天，可以聚精會神地專心一刻鐘，然後逐漸擴展，到一個月終了的時候延長到每天兩小時或兩小時以上。專心的要素，是把心靈的全部力量集中於當時正在從事的工作上面。一個人在身心疲乏的時候不能極其圓滿地做到這一點；而就兒童和年輕人的情形來說，延續太久的努力還會對於他們有所損害。

Man's Guide

by Winston Churchill[1]

MAN in this moment of his history has emerged in greater supremacy over the forces of nature than has ever been dreamed of before. There lies before him, if he wishes, a golden age of peace and progress. He has only to conquer his last and worst enemy——himself.

The only guide to a man is his conscience; the only shield to his memory is the rectitude and sincerity of his actions. It is very imprudent to walk through life without this shield, because we are so often mocked by the failure of our hopes, but with this shield, however the Fates[2] may play, we march always in the ranks of honor.

We shall go forward together. The road upward is long. There are upon our journey dark and dan-

人的指導者

在人類歷史的此一時刻，我們對於自然力量的控制能力，已經超過了人類過去所曾夢想的程度。擺在我們前面的——如果我們願意那樣的話——是一個和平與進步的黃金時代。我們每一個人所必須做的，只是征服他的最後的和最厲害的敵人——自己。

一個人的唯一的指導者是他自己的良心；他的記憶的唯一的護衛者是自己行為的正直和真誠。在人生的旅途之中行進而沒有這個護衛者，是失之輕率，因為我們常常會被希望的破滅所嘲弄；如果有這個護衛者，不論命運之神怎樣對待我們，我們永遠可以在榮譽的行列之中前進。

我們可以一起前進。向上的路是漫長的。在我們的途程上，有一些黑暗而危險的幽谷，我們必須從那裏經

gerous valleys, through which we have to <u>make and fight our way</u>[3]. But it is sure and certain that if we persevere, and we shall persevere, we shall come through these dark and dangerous valleys into a sunlight broader and more genial and more lasting than mankind has ever known.

過，而且要經過力爭苦鬥之後才能通過。但是如果我們
堅持不懈——我們將會堅持不懈的——我們必然可以通
過那些黑暗而危險的幽谷，走進一個前所未有的廣濶、
和煦、而持久的光明境界。

The Human Story

by Winston Churchill[1]

HISTORY with its flickering lamp stumbles along the trail[2] of the past, trying to reconstruct its scenes, to revive its echoes, and kindle with pale gleams the passion of former days.

As the great scroll of history unrolls, many complicated incidents occur which it is difficult to introduce effectively into the pattern of the likes and dislikes of the epoch in which we live.

The human story does not always unfold like a mathematical calculation on the principle that two and two make four. Sometimes in life they make five or minus three; and sometimes the blackboard topples down in the middle of the sum and leaves the class in disorder and the pedagogue[3] with a black eye.

人類的故事

歷史持着搖曳的燈沿着往昔的小徑蹣跚前行，試行重建往昔的景況，恢復它的迴聲，並且以灰暗的微光來點燃起昔時的熱情。

當歷史的大卷軸展開的時候，出現了許多錯綜複雜的事件，那些事件很難被適當地納入我們這個時代的人們的愛好與憎惡的範型之中。

人類的故事並非總是像數學演算一樣地按着二加二等於四的原則展現出來。在人生當中，有時候二加二等於五或負三；有時候，正演算一半，黑板突然倒塌下來，使全班陷於混亂，教師鼻青臉腫。

Science, which now offers us a golden age with one hand, offers at the same time with the other the doom[4] of all that we have built up inch by inch since the Stone Age[5] and the dawn[6] of any human annals[7]. My faith is in the high progressive destiny of man. I do not believe that we are to be flung back into abysmal[8] darkness of fiercesome discoveries which human genius has made let us make sure that they are our servants, but not our masters.

　　科學現在以一隻手奉獻給我們一個黃金時代，以另一隻手奉獻給我們一個劫數，要使我們自從石器時代以及任何人類歷史開始以來所逐漸建立起來的一切陷入萬劫不復之境。我想信，人類的命運是高超而日益向上的。我不認爲我們將被投擲到由人類天才的厲害的發明所構成的黑暗深淵之中。我們務必要主宰那些發明，而不要被那些發明所主宰。

A Better Tomorrow

by Herbert Hoover[1]

"I have but one lamp by which my feet are guided, and that is the lamp of experience."

——Patrick Henry[2]

PEOPLE often wonder why historians go to so much trouble to preserve millions of books, documents and records of the past. Why do we have libraries? What good are these documents and the history books? Why do we record and save the actions of men, the negotiations of statesmen and the campaigns of armies?

Because, sometimes, the voice of experience can cause us to stop, look and listen. And because, sometimes, past records, correctly interpreted, can give us warning of what to do and what not to do .

If we are ever to create enduring peace, we must seek its origins in human experience and in the record of human idealism. From the story of the fortitude, courage and devotion of men and women,

怎樣創造一個更好的明天

「我只有一盞明燈引導着我的脚步，那就是經驗。」

——巴特里克‧亨利

許多人常常感覺奇怪，爲什麼歷史家要那樣不辭辛勞，來保存許許多多過去的書籍、文件、和記載呢？我們爲什麼要有圖書館呢？我們爲什麼要把人們的行爲，政治家的商談，和軍隊的征戰加以記載並保存起來呢？

因爲，有時候，經驗之聲能促使我們停住脚步、觀察、和傾聽。也因爲，有時候，經過正確解釋的過去的記載，可以向我們提供一種警惕，指示我們哪些事情可以做，哪些事情不可以做。

如果我們想要創造持久的和平，我們必須從人類的經驗和理想的記載之中去探求其淵源。從男人和女人們的剛毅、勇敢、和熱誠的故事之中，我們創造了青年的

we create the inspirations of youth. From stories of
the Christian martyrs, right down to Budapest's³
heroic martyrs of today, history records the suffer-
ing, the self-denial, the denial, the devotion and the
heroic deeds of men. Surely from these records
there can come help to mankind in our confusions
and perplexities, and in our yearnings for peace.

The supreme purpose of history is a better
world. History gives a warning to those who would
promote war. History brings inspiration to those
who seek peace. In short, history helps us learn.
Yesterday's records can keep us from repeating
yesterday's mistakes. And from the pieces of
mosaic⁴ assembled by historians come the great
murals which represent the progress of mankind.

靈感。遠自基督教殉道者們的故事，近至布達佩斯當代的英勇烈士們的所做所爲，歷史在記錄着人們的一切苦難、熱誠、自我犧牲、和英勇事蹟。在我們人類今天的惶惑迷惘和對於和平的渴望之中，那些記載一定會對我們有所裨助。

　　歷史的終極目的是實現一個更好的世界。歷史對鼓動戰爭的人們加以警告。歷史對尋求和平的人們加以鼓勵。總而言之，歷史幫助我們學習。昨日的記載可以使我們避免重犯昨日的錯誤。歷史家所配集的一些鑲嵌細工，漸漸匯聚成爲表現人類進步的偉大壁畫。

Man Is Here for the Sake of Other Men

by Albert Einstein[1]

STRANGE is our situation here upon earth. Each of us comes for a short visit, not knowing why, yet sometimes seeming to <u>divine</u>[2] a purpose.

From the standpoint of daily life, however, there is one thing we do know that man is here for the sake of other men——above all for those upon whose smile and well-being our own happiness depends, and also for the countless unknown souls with whose fate we are connected by a bond of sympathy. Many times a day I realize how much my own <u>outer and inner life</u>[3] is built upon the labors of my fellow men, both living and dead, and how earnestly I must exert myself in order to give in return as much as I have received. My peace of mind is often troubled by the depressing sense that

人是爲了旁人而生活着

我們在這個世界上的處境是很奇特的。每個人都是前來做一次短暫的訪問，自己也不知道爲何而來，然而有時候卻似乎推測出一種目的。

可是，從日常生活的觀點看來，有一件事情是我們所確實知道的，那就是：人在這個世界上是爲了旁人而生活着——尤其爲了那些我們自身幸福寄託在他們的微笑和福祉之上的人們，以及那些由同情之感而使我們同他們的命運關聯起來的人們。每天都有很多次，我覺察到自己的肉體生活和精神生活是如何地建立在旁人——生者和死者都包括在內——的勞績之上，以及自己必須如何地奮發努力，以使我從旁人取得多少東西，我也可以把同等數量的東西給與旁人，藉做報答。我時常

I have <u>borrowed</u>[4] too heavily from the work of other men.

To ponder interminably over the reason for one's own existence or the meaning of life in general seems to me, from an objective point of view, to be sheer folly. And yet everyone holds certain ideals by which he guides his aspiration and his judgment. The ideals which have always shone before me and filled me with the joy of living are goodness, beauty, and truth. To make a goal of comfort and happiness has never appealed to me; a system of ethics built on this basis would be sufficient only for a herd of cattle.

懷着一種抑鬱的心情，覺得自己從旁人的工作承襲得太多，因而惴惴難安。

　　無盡無休地總在思索着自己生存的理由，或人生的意義，從客觀的觀點看起來，我覺得這似乎是極端愚蠢的行爲。可是，每個人都懷抱着一些理想，做爲他的抱負和判斷的南針。經常在我的眼前閃耀發光，並使我充滿了生之快樂的理想，就是善、美、眞。以舒適和幸福爲生活的目標，我從來無此興趣；建立在這個基礎上的一套倫理觀念，只能滿足一群牲畜的需要。

General MacArthur's[1] Prayer for His Son

BUILD me a son, O Lord, who will be strong enough to know when he is weak; and brave enough to <u>face himself</u>[2] when he is afraid; one who will be proud and unbending in honest defeat, and humble and gentle in victory.

Build me a son whose wishes will not take the place of deeds; a son who will know Thee——and that to know himself is the foundation stone of knowledge.

Lead him, I pray, not in the path of ease and comfort, but under the stress and spur of difficulties and challenge. Here let him learn to stand up in the storm; here let him learn compassion for those who fail.

Build me a son whose heart will be clean,

麥帥爲子祈禱文

主啊，請陶冶我的兒子，使他成爲一個堅強的人，能夠知道自己什麼時候是軟弱的；使他成爲一個勇敢的人，能夠在畏懼的時候認清自己，謀求補救；使他在誠實的失敗之中，能夠自豪而不屈，在獲得成功之際，能夠謙遜而溫和。

請陶冶我的兒子，使他不要以願望代替實際作爲；使他能夠認識主——並且曉得自知乃是知識的基石。

我祈求您，不要引導他走上安逸舒適的道路，而要讓他遭受困難與挑戰的磨鍊和策勵。讓他藉此學習在風暴之中挺立起來；讓他藉此學習對失敗的人們加以同情。

請陶冶我的兒子，使他的心地純潔，目標高超；在

whose goal will be high, a son who will master himself before he seeks to master other men, one who
will <u>reach into</u>[3] the future, yet never forget the past.

And after all these things are his, add, I pray
enough of a sense of humor, so that he may always
be serious, yet <u>never take himself too seriously</u>[4].
Give him humility, so that he may always remember the simplicity of true greatness, the open mind
of true wisdom, and the meekness of true strength.

Then I, his father, will dare to whisper, " I
have not lived in vain!"

企圖駕馭他人之前，先能駕馭自己；對未來善加籌畫，但是永不忘記過去。

在他把以上諸點都已做到之後，還請賜給他充分的幽默感，使他可以永遠保持嚴肅的態度，但絕不自視非凡，過於拘執。請賜給他謙遜，使他可以永遠記住真實偉大的樸實無華，真實智慧的虛懷若谷，和真實力量的溫和蘊藉。

然後，作為他的父親的我，才敢低聲說道：「我已不虛此生！」

Look Out for[1] Labels

by Joyce Cary[2]

"Not to die in the word."

I don't know who said this, but I try not to forget it. It is too easy to think we know a thing by putting a label on it. How many <u>ornithologists</u>[3] ever see a bird as a bird, <u>or botanists a flower</u>[4]?

How many politicians who legislate about children ever see the child as itself? A child is a person, good or bad, <u>usually both</u>[5], but always unique. And so are birds, flowers, trees and situations. Every moral situation is a new problem. Ask the man who runs a business, ask the woman who rules a house, ask the judge and jury at any trial.

Murder is murder. That is the label, the class, the word. But the judge wants to see the man who did it, and looking at him, asking him questions, he tries to find out what sort of a man this is, and what was his provocation. And the sentence will

切莫上了標籤的當

「不要拘泥於字面的意義。」

　　我不曉得這句話是誰說的，但是我一直把它記在心頭。為某種東西加上一個標籤，就以為我們已經曉得了它，這未免過於容易了。有多少禽鳥學家曾經認真地把一隻鳥當做鳥來看？有多少植物學家曾經認真地把一朵花當做花來看？

　　那些制定有關兒童之法律的政客們，有多少人曾經認真地把一個孩子當做孩子來看？一個孩子是一個人，也許好，也許壞，通常總是既好且壞的，但是必定是獨特的。鳥、花、樹、和情境也都如此。每一個道德的情境都是一個新問題。如果不信，你可以去問一個經營商業的男人，去問一個治理家庭的婦女，去問審理任何案件的法官和陪審員。

　　謀殺就是謀殺。那就是它的標籤，它的類別，它的名稱。但是法官想要看見那個做出謀殺行為的人，仔細地審視他，向他詢問問題，他要設法查明他是怎樣的一

depend on the answers. Justice demands a different answer for each person. One will be sent to death, and one acquitted.

Names are uniforms, they show a public fact for public use, the rank, the address, but who is the man inside? Words on the page are like the houses of a town, they make neat rows for the postman and say, "This is the town."

But the town is people. These walls of the printer's ink can hide from us the real world of individual things, each with its own beauty, of individual people, each with his own life, his own secret fears, his own private dream. They often hide him from his closest friends, his oldest enemies, even from himself.

個人，什麼原因促使他謀殺旁人。判決要視所做的回答而定。公正的法律要求每人提出不同的答覆。這一個人被判處死刑，那一個人卻被宣告無罪。

名稱像是制服，它們表明了一項共有的事實，以供大家之用，它們表明了一個階層，一個地址，但是裏面的人是誰呢？書頁上面的文字有如一個城鎮裏面的房屋，一排一排整整齊齊地擺在那裏，供郵差辨認，並且表明了：「這就是某某城鎮。」

但是那個城鎮裏面實際上是一些人。每一件東西都有它自己的美，每一個人都有他自己的生命，他自己的祕密的恐懼，他自己的私下的夢想。由印刷者的油墨所構成的牆壁，卻把那些單個東西和單個人的眞實情況完全遮蔽起來，使我們無從看見。連個人的最密切的朋友，最久遠的仇敵，甚至連他自己，都看不到他的眞實面目。

Lesson from the Moon

by Vicki Baum[1]

When the moon is fullest it begins to wane,
When it is darkest it begins to grow.

——Chinese Proverb

THERE is a calm wisdom in this old saying that impressed me when I heard it first from a monk of a Buddhist monastery in China. It has often, helped me to retain a good measure of equanimity under stress and hardship as well as when some unexpected success or good luck might have made me too exuberant. There is hope and consolation in the sure knowledge that even the darkest hours of pains and troubles won't last: but also a warning against overrating the passing glories of wealth, power and great good fortune. A warning and a hope, not only for the individual, but for governments, nations and their leaders, a brief summing up of all that history and human experience can tell us. And beyond all that we might hear in it an echo of the

月亮的教訓

「月盈則虧，晦則明。」

——中國諺語

　　這句中國的古話，最初是由佛教寺院中的一位和尚告訴我的，當時給我的印象很深。這實在是一句至理名言，蘊含着冷靜的智慧。從那時起，每當我遭逢坎坷困苦，或者遇到可能使我過於興奮的成功或好運的時候，這句話都曾幫助我保持鎮定，泰然處之。這句話提示我們，不論痛苦和憂患的時刻多麼黑暗，也不會長久持續下去，因而使我們感到希望和安慰；同時也警告我們，財富、權力、和鴻運當頭的榮耀，都只是過眼雲煙，不可過於重視。個人如此，國家和政府領袖亦然，這句箴言所提供的希望和警告，實在是整個歷史和人類經驗的結晶。除此而外，我們還可以從這句話裏面，聆聽到使

law and order that holds our universe in safe bal-
ance.

宇宙保持平衡狀態的法律與秩序的回聲。

Truth Is for Everyone

by Rabindranath Tagore[1]

THERE are some people, who are proud and wise and practical, who say that it is not in human nature to be generous, that men will always fight one another, that the strong will conquer the weak, and that there can be no real moral foundation for man's civilization. We cannot deny the facts of their assertion that the strong have power in the human world, but I refuse to accept this as a revelation of truth······

We should know that truth, any truth that man acquires, is for everyone. Money and property belong to individuals, to each of you, but you must never exploit truth for your personal ag-grandizement[2]; that would be selling God's blessing for a profit. However, science is also truth; it has

眞理是爲一切人而設的

有一些很自尊，很明智，很切實的人們，他們說，寬厚並不是人類的本性，人們將永遠互相鬥爭，強者將把弱者征服，人類的文明不會有眞實的道德基礎。他們所說的強者在人類世界上具有權勢，乃是事實，我們無從否認，但是我不能把這種說法當做眞理的啓示而加以接受。……

我們應該知道，眞理——人類所獲得的任何眞理——是爲一切人而設的。金錢和財產屬於個人，屬於你們當中的每一個人，但是你們絕對不可利用眞理來增長你們個人的財富和權勢；因爲那樣做就等於出賣上帝的恩澤，藉以牟利。可是科學也是眞理；它的適當的職分

its place in the healing of the sick, and in giving more food and leisure for life. When it helps the strong crush the weak, and rob those who are asleep, it is using truth for <u>impious</u>[3] ends. Those who are thus <u>sacrilegious</u>[4] will suffer and be punished, for their own weapons will <u>be turned against</u>[5] them.

在於醫療病人，爲人類生命提供更多的養料與休閒。如果它幫助強者去壓服弱者，去掠奪那些在沈睡中的人們，它就是在利用眞理去達成不虔敬的目的。那些以這種方式褻瀆神聖的人們必將受到報應和懲罰，因爲他們的武器將被用以對付他們本身。

True Nobility

by Ernest Hemingway[1]

IN a calm sea every man is a pilot.

But all sunshine without shade, all pleasure without pain, is not life at all. Take the lot of the happiest——it is a tangled yarn. Bereavements and blessings, one following another, make us sad and blessed by turns[2]. Even death itself makes life more loving. Men come closest to their true selves in the sober moments of life, under the shadows of sorrow and loss.

In the affairs of life or of business, it is not intellect that tells[3] so much as character, not brains so much as heart, not genius so much as self-control, patience, and discipline, regulated by judgment.

I have always believed that the man who has

眞實的高貴

在一個風平浪靜的海面上，每個人都可以做一個駕船的人。

但是，如果只有陽光而無陰影，只有快樂而無痛苦，那便全然不是人生。即以最幸福的人的遭際來說——那也無異於一團纏結的紗線。親人死亡和快樂幸福，一椿接着一椿地連續而來，使我們一陣悲愁，一陣愉快。甚至連死亡本身都會使人生更加親切。在人生當中的冷靜時刻，在悲哀和喪失的暗影之下，人們最接近他們的眞實的自我。

在人生或職務的各種事項之中，智力所發生的作用，沒有性格大；頭腦所發生的作用，不如心情；天才所發生的作用，不如由判斷力所節制着的自制、耐心、和戒律。

begun to live more seriously within begins to live more simply without. In an age of extravagance and waste, I wish I could show to the world how few the real wants of humanity are.

To regret one's errors to the point of not repeating them is true repentance. There is nothing noble in being superior to some other man. The true nobility is in being superior to your previous self.

我始終認為，一個人如果已經開始在內心裏生活得更為嚴肅，便會開始在外表上生活得更為簡樸。在一個奢侈浪費的時代之中，我但願我能向世人表明，人類所真正需要的東西是如何的微少。

悔恨自己的錯誤，而達到不重犯那些錯誤的地步，這是真實的悔悟。比旁人強，並沒有什麼高貴之處。比以前的自己強，才是真實的高貴。

Courage

by John F. Kennedy[1]

THE courage of life is often a less dramatic spectacle than the courage of a final moment; but it is no less a magnificent mixture of triumph and tragedy. A man does what he must——in spite of[2] personal consequences, in spite of obstacles and dangers and pressures——and that is the basis of all human morality.

To be courageous······requires no exceptional qualifications, no magic formula, no special combination of time, place and circumstance. It is an opportunity that sooner or later[3] is presented to us all. Politics merely furnishes one arena[4] which imposes special tests of courage. In whatever arena of life one may meet challenge of courage, whatever may be the sacrifices he faces if he follows his con-

勇　氣

　　在人生當中所表現的勇氣，看起來往往不如在最後關頭所表現的勇氣那麼富於戲劇性；但是這種勇氣卻同樣是勝利和悲劇的一個壯麗的混合體。一個人去做他必須做的事情——不顧個人的後果，不顧種種的障礙、危險、和壓力——這就是一切人類道德的基礎。

　　勇敢……並不需要什麼非常的條件，不需要什麼奇妙的定律，也不需要時間、地點、和情勢的特殊配合。勇敢乃是我們每人遲早都會遇到的一個機會。政治不過是對於我們的勇氣加以嚴苛考驗的許多活動範圍之一而已。不論我們將在人生的哪一個活動範圍之中去應付勇氣的挑戰，不論我們爲了遵從自己的良知而將面對着怎

science——the loss of his friends, his fortune,his contentment, even the esteem of his fellow men ——each man must decide for himself the course he will follow. The stories of past courage can define that ingredient——they can teach, they can offer hope,they can provide inspiration. But they cannot supply courage itself. For this each man must look into his own soul.

樣的犧牲——朋友、財產、和滿足的喪失，甚至旁人對你的敬重的喪失——每個人都必須自行決定他所將採取的方針。旁人的勇敢的故事可以闡釋那個因素——那些故事能夠教導我們，為我們帶來希望和靈感，但是不能把勇氣本身帶給我們。勇氣這種東西，每個人必須到自己的靈魂裏面去尋求。

NOTES

- *On the Exercise of One's Mental Perception*
  1. Plutarch (46?-120? A. D.)——Greek biographer and moralist.
  2. come in its way——within its reach; encounter it.
  3. make after——attempt to catch.
  4. emulation——ambition or desire to equal or excel.

- *The Golden Mean*
  1. the golden mean——the safe, prudent, way between extremes.
  2. Balthasar Gracian是西班牙的一位天主教耶穌會神父，也是一位文人，生於十六世紀末，死於1658年。
  3. do violence to——inflict injury upon; outrage.

- *On the Instability of Human Glory*
  1. 狄福(1660?－1731)——英國小說家，「魯濱遜漂流記」之作者。
  2. fame——public report.
  3. take up——occupy; fill.

4. eternity——immortality.

- *Monuments in Westminster Abbey*

    1. Westminster Abbey——a large Gothic church in London, England: the burial place of English monarchs, outstanding statesmen, famous writers.

    2. Joseph Addison (1672—1719)——English essayist and poet.

    3. inordinate desire——immoderate wish.

    4. kings lying by those who deposed them —— in Henry VII's Chapel in Westminster Abbey, Mary Queen of Scots lies not far from her gaoler and executioner, Queen Elizabeth.

    5. rival wits——Addison, the great wit on the Whig side, and Prior, his contemporary, one of the great wits on the Tory side, lies near each other.

    6. that great day——Judgment Day, the time of God's final judgment of all people; end of the world; doomsday.

- *Affectation*
  1. affectation——the use of unnatural or artificial manners, speech, or behavior.
  2. 柴斯菲爾勳爵（即Philip Dormer Stanhope. 1694-1773）——英國政治家及作家。
  3. nature——the force or agency that seems to regulate the entire universe, acting as a creative, guiding, intelligence.
  4. preponderate——weigh more than something else.
  5. counterpoise——a weight which counterbalances another.
  6. vanity——being excessively proud of one's own merit.
  7. observation——remark.
- *Comparison*
  1. 休姆(1711－1776)——英國哲學家與歷史家。
  2. in the nature of things——in the regular order or constitution of the universe.
  3. the one——the former.
  4. the other——the latter.

- *National Prejudices*

  1. 高爾斯密(1728－1774)──英國詩人，戲劇家，小說家。

  2. antiquity──the early period of history, especially before the Middle Ages.

  3. the philosopher──指Socrates.

  4. profession──declaration.

  5. comprehend──include.

  6. Did these prejudices prevail──If these prejudices prevailed.

  7. this appellation──指gentleman.

  8. make bold──dare; be so bold as.

- *On the Fear of Death*

  1. William Hazlitt (1778－1830)──English critic and essayist.

  2. when we were not──when we did not exist.

  3. to be──to exist.

  4. Queen Anne(1665－1714)──queen of Great Britain and Ireland from 1702 to 1714.

  5. lay it so much to heart──lay to heart＝be deeply affected by or concerned about; think

seriously about.

6. disburthening——disburdening.

7. the stage of life——Cf. AS YOU LIKE IT, II. vii. 139−143: "All the world's a stage, And all the men and women merely players: They have their exits and their entrances; And one man in his time plays many parts, His acts being seven ages." (William Shakespeare)

8. perdus——lost.

9. nonage——early stage.

● *Companionship of Books*

1. 史邁爾斯(1812−1904)——英國作家。

2. turn one's back upon——repulse; forsake; refuse to acknowledge.

3. by far——加強最高級形容詞the most lasting之意義。

4. of no account——trifling; insignificant.

5. mind——person having intelligence or regarded as an intellectual.

6. in a measure——somewhat; to some extent.

● *The Cynic*

1. Cynic——犬儒派哲學家；犬儒主義者。Cynic源於一個希臘字，其義爲「狗」，因爲此派哲學家認爲自然的生活——沒有財產、習俗和其他人爲的複雜關係的限制，像狗的生活一般——是最好的生活。犬儒學派是由希臘哲學家Antisthenes創始的，其主要學說是認爲美德是唯一的善，而美德的要素則是自制；並且輕蔑逸樂、金錢、和安適。此一學派的信徒對於社會上其他的人們持着一種指摘的態度，認爲人們一切行爲的動機莫不出於自私。Antisthenes的弟子Diogenes住在桶中，白天提着燈籠到各處尋覓誠實的人，可以算是犬儒派哲學家的典範。Cynic的意義漸指「憤世嫉俗者」（作此義解時第一個字母小寫）。

2. Henry Ward Beecher (1813－1887)——美國牧師及演說家。

3. mousing for——hunting for; seeking about or searching for something.

4. game——animals and birds hunted for sport and food.

5. innuendo——an indirect suggestion against somebody.

6. green——not trained or experienced; not

mature in age, judgment, etc.

- *Riches*
  1. Henry Ward Beecher (1813－1887)——美國牧師及演說家。
  2. rear——erect by building.
  3. almoner——person who distributes alms or charhity.

- *Poverty*
  1. Henry Ward Beecher (1813－1887)——美國牧師及演說家。
  2. howling wilderness——one full of wild bests; dreary wilderness.
  3. bicker——squabble.
  4. satiety——the feeling of having had too much; satiated condition.

- *The Time Is Short*
  1. Philips Brooks (1835－1893)——American clergyman.
  2. run on——keep on; continue.
  3. ache for——have a longing for.
  4. break the spell——do away with misunder-

standings.

- *Irony and Pity*

1. irony——the expression of one's meaning by saying something which is the direct opposite of one's thoughts, in order to make one's remarks forceful.

2. 法朗士(1844－1924)——法國小說家及諷刺家。

3. Goddess Isis——an Egyptian goddess of motherhood and fertility, sister and wife of Osiris, represented with a cows's horns and the sun's disk as a crown. The tears of Goddess Isis which fall into the Nile, cause the inundation of the river, and thus bring to the land abundance, wealth, and the means of nourishment.

4. Goddess Nephthys——an Egyptian goddess, daughter of Geb and Nut, sister and wife of Set, who with Isis was especially associated with the ritual of the dead.

5. of good counsel——offering good advice.

6. but for——if it were not for.

- *Man and Nature*
    1. Hamilton Wright Mabie(1846－1916──美國編輯
       人，批評家，散文家。
    2. To Nature we turn ── turn to: go to for as-
       sistance.
    3. spent──tired out; exhausted.
    4. appealing──being attractive, interesting, etc.;
       arousing a favorable response.
    5. unsuspected──not imagined to be existent,
       probable, etc.
- *The Mission of the Motion Picture*
    1. 愛迪生(1847－1931)──美國發明家。
    2. at best──taking the most hopeful view.
    3. on the average──as an average rate.
    4. next to──almost.
- *We Are on a Journey*
    1. 戴克(1852－1933)──美國傳教士，演說家與作家。
    2. at rest──in repose.
    3. childlike──innocent; simple.
    4. childish──immature; silly; not fit for an
       adult.

- *The Strenuous Life*

    1. 提奧多・羅斯福(1858－1919)──美國第二十六任總統。

    2. save──except.

    3. to good purpose──with good effect; very successfully.

    4. thrice──very; greatly.

    5. to take rank with──to have the same rank as.

- *Concentration*

    1. George Allardice Riddell (1865－1934)──英國新聞事業家。

    2. not...any more than──used to exclude or deny a second clause equally with a first.

    3. in these days──nowadays.

    4. in hand──being worked on; receiving attention.

- *Man's Guide*

    1. 邱吉爾(1874－1965)──英國政治家與作家，第二次大戰期間任英國首相，1953 年諾貝爾文學獎之得主。

    2. Fates──希臘神話中司命運之三女神，即Clotho, Lachesis, Atropos.

3. make one's way——advance; proceed.

    fight one's way——advance by struggles or conflicts; overcome difficulties.

- *The Human Story*

1. 邱吉爾(1874－1965)——英國政治家與作家。

2. trail——path.

3. pedagogue——schoolmaster; teacher.

4. doom——tragic fate; ruin or death.

5. the Stone Age——period of culture when weapons and tools were made of stone (before the use of metals was known).

6. dawn——beginning.

7. annals——history.

8. abysmal——like an abyss; bottomless.

- *A Better Tomorrow*

1. 胡佛(1874－1964)——美國第三十一任總統。

2. 巴特里克・亨利(1797－1878)——美國的愛國者，演說家。此語係出自他的一篇著名演說Speech in the Virginia Convention。

3. Budapest為匈牙利首都。此處所述，指匈牙利之反共抗暴運動。

4. mosaic——work of art in which designs, pictures, etc. are made by fitting together differently colored bits of stone, glass, etc.

- *Man Is Here for the Sake of Other Men*

1. 愛因斯坦(1879－1955)——生於德國之美國物理學家，為相對論之發明者。

2. divine——find out by intuition or insight; conjecture.

3. outer life——physical life.

   inner life——spiritual or mental life.

4. borrowed——adopted or taken over as one's own.

- *General MacArthur's Prayer for His Son*

1. 麥克阿瑟(1880－1964)——美國將軍。麥克阿瑟將軍曾對美國西點軍校學生發表一篇演說，題目是 "Duty, Honor and Country." 其內容大致與本文相同。因此他這篇「為子祈禱文」的內容，不僅是他對於他的兒子的期許，也是他用以訓勉美國軍校學生以至全體美國青年的箴言；換句話說，也就是他自己所服膺的做人原則。

2. face himself——see himself as he is and rem-

edy his shortcomings.

3. reach into——plan for.

4. never take himself too seriously——be flexible, open to suggestions, etc.

- *Look Out for Labels*

    1. look out for——be on the watch for.

    2. Joyce Cary (1888－1957)——英國小說家與詩人。

    3. ornithologist——person who studies or who knows much about birds.

    4. or botanists a flower＝or botanists ever see a flower as a flower.

    5. usually both＝usually both good and bad.

- *Lesson from the Moon*

    1. Vicki Baum (1888－1960)——American novelist.

- *Truth Is for Everyone*

    1. 泰戈爾(1891－1941)——印度詩人，曾獲 1913 年諾貝爾文學獎。

    2. aggrandizement——increase in power, position, riches, etc.

    3. impious——not have reverence for God; wicked.

4. sacrilegious——injurious or insulting to sacred persons or things.

5. be turned against——be used to the disadvantage or injury of.

- *True Nobility*

1. 海明威(1898－1961)——美國小說家。

2. by turns——one after another; alternately.

3. tell——produce a result; be effective.

- *Courage*

1. 甘迺迪(1917－1963)——美國第三十五任總統。本文摘自他所著的Profiles in Courage（中文本譯爲「當仁不讓」）一書。

2. in spite of——not to be prevented by; notwithstanding,

3. sooner or later——some time or other.

4. arena——any sphere of struggle or exertion.

英語散文集錦

萬卷文庫 61

編 譯 者：吳奚真

創 辦 人：姚宜瑛

發 行 人：吳錫清

主 　 編：張清志

封面設計：張佑維

法律顧問：余淑杏律師

出 版 者：大地出版社

台北市內湖區環山路三段 26 號 1 樓

劃撥帳號：0019252－9

電話：（02）2627－7749

傳真：（02）2627－089

印刷者：松霖彩色印刷公司

初版：中華民國八十四年一月

初版二刷：中華民國八十八年十二月

定 　 價：150 元

ISBN：957－9460－51－5

Printed in Taiwan